The Memory of Water

Jack Myers

New Issues Poetry & Prose

A Green Rose Book

New Issues Poetry & Prose
The College of Arts and Sciences
Western Michigan University
Kalamazoo, Michigan 49008

Copyright© 2011 by Jack Myers. All rights reserved.
Printed in the United States of America.

First Edition, 2011.

ISBN-10:	1-930974-98-1 (paperbound)
ISBN-13:	978-1-930974-98-2 (paperbound)

Library of Congress Cataloging-in-Publication Data:
Myers, Jack
The Memory of Water/Jack Myers
Library of Congress Control Number: 2010940517

Art Direction:	Tricia Hennessy
Design:	The Design Center
Cover Image:	Peter Feldman
Production:	Paul Sizer
	The Design Center, Frostic School of Art
	College of Fine Arts
	Western Michigan University
Printing:	McNaughton & Gunn, Inc.

The Memory of Water

Jack Myers

New Issues
WESTERN MICHIGAN UNIVERSITY

Also by Jack Myers

Poetry:

Routine Heaven
The Glowing River: New & Selected Poems
OneOnOne
Blindsided
Human Being
As Long as You're Happy
Coming to the Surface
I'm Amazed That You're Still Singing
The Family War
Will It Burn
Black Sun Abraxas

Nonfiction:

The Poet's Portable Workshop
Dictionary of Poetic Terms
Leaning House Poets, Vol. 1
New American Poets of the 90's
A Profile of Twentieth-Century American Poetry
The Longman Dictionary of Poetic Terms
A Trout in the Milk: A Composite Portrait of Richard Hugo
New American Poets of the 80's

For my son, Jacob Myers, 1985-2009

Contents

	Foreword by Mark Cox	5
	Cirrus	11
I.	The Sum of One's Parts	
	Black Loam	15
	The Archer	16
	Necklace of Moss	17
	Really Fast Chicken	18
	Sleep Walking	19
	Hairy Legs and Ugly Woman's Feet	20
	Doggie's Day Out	21
	Wake-Up Call	22
	The Story of Me	23
	The Whole Being Larger than the Sum of Its Parts	24
	Snapshots of Prague	25
	Invisible Stones	26
	Blumenthal's	27
	Dark Matter	28
	Here and There	29
	Stone Koan	30
	Treasure Hunt	31
	Calling	32
	Paradise	33
	You Are What You Don't Eat	34
	Lion Kings	35
	Life on Earth	36
	Cloud, Backlit	37
II.	Shell Game	
	Same Sea	41
	My Life	42
	Golden Watch	43
	Riding Shotgun in My Life	44
	Art	45
	There is Nothing in My Hands	46
	The Art of Living	47
	Bucket Heads	48
	Catwalk, Flag Part, Tent Flap, Shoe Tongue	49
	Cardinal Rules	50
	Study: Imitation Long Grass with Nest	51
	Shell Game	52
	B-Movie	53
	One Last Wish	55

	Extracting the Essence	56
	Nose Job	57
	Human Flames	58
	Wild Onions	59
	Mariscos	61
	In	63
	Stupid Human Tricks	64
	Mean Streak	65
	Unstable	66
	Intimacies of Cleaning	67
	Fragments	68
	Any Minute Now	69
	Helpmeet	70
	Still Smoldering	71
III.	Beggar's Cup	
	Past Due	75
	Birth Day Party	76
	Going Away Party	77
	Someone Else's Shoes	78
	Home	79
	Paean against Pain	80
	In the Dark	81
	Eating Grief	82
	Renovation	83
	Wall of Absence	84
	Neither Here nor There	85
	To-Do List	86
	Usually and mostly	87
	The World's Highest Mountain	88
	When the Angel Came for Him	89
	Beggar's Cup	90
	The Amnesiac's Memoir	91
	The Golden Years	92
	What the Old Master Said	93
	Cholangiocarcinoma	94
	Every Thing	95
	American Bardo	96
	Grave Question	97
	String Theory	98
	This	99
	Plans	100
	Desert is the Memory of Water	101
	Road Work	102

Foreword

Jack Myers (1941-2009) was a superb poet and a special man. His recent passing has been a great loss to the multitude of friends, students and fellow poets who loved him and his work. Over his thirty-four years as a teacher at Southern Methodist University and Vermont College, Jack influenced the lives of countless writers. Never the type to phone it in, he was specific in his critical advice and supportive of his students' growth. In the twenty-six years I knew him, his progressive evolution as a poet, thinker, and human being were a continual inspiration to me. And he brought that sense of ongoing exploration and hope into every classroom he entered, right to the end. We were fortunate enough to host him at the University of North Carolina, Wilmington, in 2008. It was the last group of students with which he would ever interact and he enjoyed every minute of his time with them. Even when his illness grew most severe, he never failed to ask after those writers and the department as a whole. We were a culminating moment for him—a bright spot prior to his tragic physical decline. I know it was important to him to feel he had done right by us, that he had laced up his work boots and given his students all he had to give.

For my part, I can say that Jack was such an integral part of my life, I genuinely can't imagine what would have happened to me had we not met. I have had no more important teacher, colleague or friend. Over the past twenty-five years, I have co-taught with dozens of first-rate, prominent poets—and I have never known a more perceptive, knowledgeable, or generous teacher than Jack. But first and foremost, he was an extraordinary poet who was unswervingly committed to his art for forty years.

*

Jack wasn't born into an academic environment. He grew up in the '40s and '50s, in the blue-collar community of Winthrop, MA, influenced by hard-working Jewish parents. He said he knew, however, from the age of twelve, that poetry gave him access to an inner self and knowledge. Rebellious and argumentative in his twenties, Jack was a poet-vagabond. Even as he gradually found his way to the University of Massachusetts, Boston, and Iowa for degrees, married and took on family responsibilities, he worked many service and menial jobs, including lobsterman and housepainter. That he first experienced poetry in life outside the University is made very clear in his work.

Ultimately, Jack's poetry mentor was Richard Hugo, himself a student of Theodore Roethke, so it is no surprise that Jack's poetry reflects an intentional, but submerged formality, an adherence to the conversational mode, and an abiding commitment to the exploration of self and spirit in the material world. His insistence on the presence of the extraordinary within the ordinary, his unique mixture of humor, working-class sensibility and spiritual ambition was ground-breaking and influenced many poets of my generation who began coming up in the early '80s. Their desire to meld street smarts, quotidian subject matter and quicksilver diction with higher existential explorations followed on the heels of poets like Jack and Bill Matthews. Like Matthews, he was always drawn to bringing the grandiose down to earth and at the same time elevating all deemed merely ordinary to the prominence it truly held in our lives—something sublime and greater than ourselves and our own brief time.

In Jack's case, his fusion of Eastern mysticism, Jungian psychology, and contemporary American domestic life was unique. Over the years, using therapy and spiritual study, he forced old angsts and regrets into a sense of ongoing exploration and hope. He forged better relationships. He freely shared his mistakes and embarrassments with students. He grew more open, tolerant and wise.

*

The burgeoning community of writing programs has created self-sustaining biospheres of poets and audience. On the positive side, this sustains the art during a period when the national culture disregards it. One of the dangers, however, is that within these subcultures, we can gradually become myopic. We begin to write for each other, for crass reward, or in service of narrow ideas. We lose touch with the driven, soulful ambitions our great writers have always aspired to.

In recent years, one major trend has been a poetry characterized by radical disjuncture, strategic non sequitur, extreme yoking of disparate elements of high and low culture, very clever wordplay, and a general distrust of narrative and figurative language. The rejection of sentiment is crucial to these writers; they do not want to look foolish or old-fashioned, and they don't want to risk being direct, let alone sordid.

These are understandable aesthetic hesitations. The most ambitious and talented of these poets genuinely seek to challenge traditional assumptions about unity and structure. They lament that much contemporary poetry has become complacent about the democratized aesthetic culture of the post-war era, too often over-zealous in its celebration of its liberation from intellect, and often disallowing cerebral intelligence altogether. These mainstream poems can and do become simplistic, relying on their subjects for effect, instead of becoming well-wrought works of art that engage readers in the enactment of experience.

On the other hand, though stylistic dissonance, inconsistency, and fragmentation may be aesthetically appropriate to the era we live in, the peer pressures of fashion too often result in skeletal imitations. This formal resistance becomes an expectation, no more valid than a metrical scheme or the formulaic free verse lyric that it is challenging. In essence, the style becomes content, which leads to self-referential elitism, parlor games of ideology based in intellectual generalities rather than particular emotional or psychological intimacies.

*

Jack appreciated, and would never have argued against, elliptical, impressionistic, surreal and generally difficult, innovative poetries. Nor would he have argued that poetry has to be autobiographical in order to be successful. He knew it has everything to do with the poet's level of engagement and ambition. The loss of differentiation between the terms confessional, autobiographical and personal has not helped matters here. I think Jack would have said that poems need not be confessional or autobiographical, but that poems he valued were always personal. Jack insisted that no matter how intrusive or effaced the poem's organizing sensibility might be, it should reflect genuine necessity—be it emotional, psychological or intellectual.

Jack felt that poetry, no matter what the aesthetic style, always has a larger responsibility and requires our complete investment in it. It's not about the advertising potential of Facebook and Goodreads. It's not enough to make ironic observations, pose obtuse questions or merely list events. The act of writing is to explore, with depth and dimension, why and how the poem and its subject matter have come to pass, what it may have to do with the future, and, most importantly, how it reflects the poet's evolving relationship with the world.

Critics who dismissed Jack for being insular just didn't perceive how immense and open the inner world of his narrator actually was. He was always highly conscious of living in direct relation to the lives of others around him. He accepted the chaotic fluidity of experience, as well as the need to create some kind of symmetry from that flux. He did not shirk our human responsibility to create meaning from uncertainty and to exist spiritually in those uncertainties that we can barely contend with.

*

Earlier, I said that I don't know what my life would have been like, had I not met Jack. This is not an overstatement. Without fanfare, overlooked between West and East Coast publishing, he produced some of the most valuable poetry of his generation. He showed me just how insignificant the career and ego issues of poetry really are. He showed me that to write seriously is to live seriously, and with an abiding, ever-deepening attention to the past and an increasing sense of responsibility for the future. One comes to terms with things; one doesn't go around the self, you go through it, you work your way through it. And that's why the great poets, the poets that we can turn to again and again, both for provocative thought and solace, gift us with bodies of work—progressions through which we can experience their personal journeys.

The book you hold is the closing chapter of Jack's journey. Jack's illness kept him from reorganizing the manuscript in accordance with a new title and concept. In consultation with Jack's widow, Thea Temple, who knows Jack's inclinations and wishes better than anyone, I have tried to organize this final book in a way that would please him. This version includes late poems and stragglers from his files that I believe enhance the book, even though he did not plan to include them. In a very few cases, I have polished poems that I feel he would have finished, had he lived to do so. Again, in consultation with Thea, whose contributions have been numerous and crucial, I revised as lightly and as near to Jack's original intentions as I could.

This book has seemed a living entity to me. Jack's voice has been in the air for months. I have tried hard to listen and to make the right choices without imposing too much of myself. It is my hope that this book will offer Jack's many fans an enactment of the tensions and energies flowing through his last years. I hope, too, that it will welcome many new readers into an appreciation of the whole of his poetry, which is a remarkably consistent and brilliant body of work.

Mark Cox
University of North Carolina, Wilmington
September, 2010

Cirrus

*I'd like to leave
an imprint
on the world
lighter than
I'd formerly meant.
Just a scent,
not the thud
of the thing
steaming on a plate.*

*Instead of "I told you so!"
let my epitaph be
the glance, the edge,
the mist. The delicately
attenuated swirl
of an innuendo
instead of the thunderhead.*

*The rain that fell
when I was ambitious
seemed conspiringly rushed
in my way. But the same rain
today tastes of here and now
because of where it's been.*

*I'd like to be gentle
with small, great things.
They are larger
than what we think
we came here for.
I'd like to be an eye of light
that opens the air
and burns beyond ambition,
like the sun that can't see us
and is beyond our human reach,
yet is in us trillions of times over.*

I. The Sum of One's Parts

When all things return to One
even gold loses its value.
But when the One returns to all things
even the pebbles sparkle.

—Zen saying

Black Loam

It's been another good year.
I pitchfork my poems into the air
over and over until the black grains
of letters pile up into never before

thought of things. All winter I'll pound them
into dust and bake from that the black bread
of meaning which is leavened by death
and is its source and devourer.

After I've winnowed the poems, the wind
will seem to have blown the seeds
right out of oblivion. But it is only taking life
from life, the many from the one, which is how
I came to be and is what I have done.

The Archer

Each day only a sliver or two of awareness
flies into my amorphous consciousness
to nestle in the dreaming self
I'll soon be sleeping deeper in.

And each night I dream I'm shooting
like a star into the distance of the same next day
even as it's being scribbled over
with mistakes and countless changes.

I sharpen my face into a third eye,
pull back everything I am,
then let go and vanish
beyond an invisible point of no return.

I've lived my whole life this way.
There is no target.

Necklace of Moss

Remember the old blue dory a storm coughed up,
how you packed its seams with tar-soaked caulking
and painted it blue so you couldn't be seen very easily—
blue on blue under blue—how that's what you wanted?

You with your adolescent thoughts of killing yourself
hooked so deep, pickerel boy, you never believed
you'd grow old. Can you see me now? I am the ocean
you rowed across. The sun tanning you golden is me.
My life is yours.

Let's scare ourselves today and go really far out
just to see what we're made of. We'll beach the boat
and scrape off the moss that's been slowing it down.
We'll do it in honor of having gone so far out that
we became possible, something we thought we could never be.

Really Fast Chicken

In my dreams of flying
I lay out in the air and glide
merely by feeling I'd like to.

That's what I thought it'd be like
to be a poet when I was 12—dumb-struck
by daydreams, my hand would write.

But real birds sweat when they fly.
In slo-mo it appears they're rowing
the longboat of their bodies

across vast tracts of invisible swells
with nothing to land on, except
the twig of a dream of being us.

Impossible adaptation, growing wings.
I picture a really fast chicken
launching himself into the blue

safety of nothing as if wanting itself
could buoy him up, as if faith in what
he didn't know would pull him forward,

as if saying would save his life, and dreaming
arctic arias and flaunting jungle colors
would make it impossible to fall.

Sleep Walking

Sometimes I lose touch with myself
and my life seems like a dream I inhabit
until the dream inhabits me, a mirror
I stare into without reflection, as if I were
a go-between invisibly doing what's required
of me without knowing what's required of me.

I think I'm like my dog who's going deaf
and accepts living inside the stillness
of a thing that doesn't know what it is
while the world grows brighter than
the one I'm in which I suspect has become
a replica of what I've come to expect.

Still, from within my caul of raptness
I'm dumbfounded by flowers. How
could seeds imagine these? Colors as subtle
as dreams, as rarified as prayers, fragrances
with an openness that rises beyond the sexual
so the world's transformed by grace. Stunned,

I watch all this without having any sense
of my part in it, like the murder mysteries
I love to cleverly second-guess in which
the unthinkable pollinates the possible
and blooms into the gorgeous sweetness of an
ah-ha moment and leaves me wondering
what's next, fruit!?

Hairy Legs and Ugly Woman's Feet

When I took my wife and daughter for a pedicure
I ended up in a massage chair getting my toenails
painted "Carrot Red." I had to laugh with them,
looking at my hairy legs and ugly woman's feet.

And when I turned 65, I got my right ear pierced
only to find out too late, there's a secret code that says
"right is wrong," unless you're gay and underneath
you happen to be stifling the urge to wear a housedress.

Ok, I'll admit when I saw my butt in the mirror once
I thought it was cute. Ok, I even imagined passing myself
and looking back. And I admit I'm jealous of my wife's
unmentionables which look like an assortment of Popsicles.

But the woman in me I'm freeing doesn't care what people think.
She got an unexpected boost when I was lounging with the ladies
in what must've looked like a harem chamber when a teenager
walked by and gave me the big thumbs-up. That was so unreal

he could've been my guardian angel. But my wife saw him too.
I whispered "Live as if you were dead" to myself, meaning
what dead guy wouldn't give both legs to come back to
this paradise-on-earth and have his toenails painted red?

Doggie's Day Out

> *Because we are also what we have lost.*
> —from the movie *Amores Perros*

The door to the world opens
and my dog and I take a walk.
He's tiny so he has to trot
to keep up, much like me.
With his wolf's heart he listens,
sniffs, and pisses on each mailbox,
even after his ambition, like mine,
is long out of ammunition.

There's nothing dangerous here,
I laugh at him. A little old lady groomer
pinned a pretty pink bow on his head
where it floats like a clichéd thought.
He doesn't understand humiliation
because he and his image of himself
are so solidly in coincidence he sees things
in black and white, literally. He asks
am I welcome here or not?

To him the old man sweeping the sunset
behind the hills comes directly from
the default archetypal forest of his heart
where discretion and attack play leap frog
over bogs of sleep. We are brothers
with the wilderness gone out of us.
The world once beyond the end
of my thumb and his black nose
is now inside us. Everything we've lived
is now part of us, and this new forgetting
and confusion is the beginning of giving
it all back, becoming everything, the whole
unspooling ribbon and blur is itself a thing
of beauty. I pin a pink bow on it. It goes
through me in one long continuous shock
of recognition though it's only a walk around the block.

Wake-Up Call

> *You're afraid that you may not be the dying leader you thought you were, or that your death may be as meaningless as everyone else's.*
> —Admiral Adama, *Battlestar Galactica*

I don't imagine lesser beings
such as ants worry about their sense
of purpose since it's buried
so deep inside the blindness of
their natural single-mindedness.

Maybe they can't lift it up like a problem,
like us, and turn it around in the light of reason,
but unlike us they're what's lifted up by it.

Haven't you always had the feeling there's
Something Else You're Supposed To Be
Doing? Haven't you tried to trick yourself
into realizing it, like trying to catch yourself
blinking in the mirror, while it's watching you
the way you idly watch an ant? Maybe it's
something no one's discovered yet like *Restless
Leg Syndrome*, which only restlessness can treat.

Maybe this is just me not accepting stage one of
End-of-life Crisis Syndrome, which, take my word for it,
with all the money dying Baby Boomers have,
some charlatan will prove real in single-blind
experiments. I know my wife and I often have the same
thought at the exact same time, we just can't tell
who's transmitting and who's receiving. I've certified
myself through self-study to examine stuff like this.

You know that pure electronic tone that blooms in your head
as if you were receiving an emergency broadcast signal?
Couldn't that be the wake-up call for having another purpose?
I've seen auguries everywhere that are telling me to start over.
But look at the progress I've already made: I've discovered
that my life's work is to discover my real life's work.

The Story of Me

When I set out to make my way,
I wanted my journey to be short.
But it turned out long,
made of thousands of shorter journeys.

Along the way my name fell off,
my words broke into crumbs.
I was a film in a projector, stuck
between light and the simple bliss of being,
and everything I saw of the story was me.

That's different than in The Story of Enlightenment,
in which everything sees The Story of Me.
I was still all ego, the little, star-struck fish
who spent his whole life questing for
the miraculous thing called water,
whose journey, if he had just let it be,
would've been a heel click in the air,
happier than I ever was.

The Whole Being Larger than the Sum of Its Parts

I can almost sense the shape of my life, as if its
moments were being poured and cooled into an ingot.

Compared to the force that's doing this,
my sense of purpose is merely a hardened color.

It's difficult being your own medium, like iron
trying to wrest itself into a magnet,

like memory flooding down blind alleys
looking for the word on the tip of your tongue.

When will my sixth sense kick in and finally be able
to put its arms around the life I'm living?

My awareness seems to be the air around this thing.
I wouldn't be asking if I were just this thing.

Snapshots of Prague

Immaculate white swans float in the river's
fishless dishwater like squat question marks.

Under the huge stone buildings,
looking like sunken wedding cakes,
lovers kiss and grow shells of longing over themselves,

as if dreariness decided to imagine them
as pink and purple petals of amnesia
growing out of something long and terrible.

At dinner, a waitress charges me $10
for a bottle of water without blinking.
When I complain she looks me in the eye
as if to say cost can be a ladder out of loss.

Next morning on the tram a well-dressed man
whose eyes are white gets up. Then his wife,
who is also blind takes his arm, and they get off.
I close my eyes to feel what it is like to be her
following the sound of tapping my way home.

I've set the camera to snap a picture of me
under a portico of gods and caryatids. I have no idea
where I really am. But I could never be from here.
Then again I think, why not? I'm always trying to catch up to
where I'm at. I've always felt I can't be where I'm from.

Invisible Stones

The house I will build from the forest
in my retirement will overlook
a lake, and be a huddle of adobe
with candle and incense holders
and Arabian rugs and oriental screens
and a porthole or two for a clock.

The ivy-covered house I live in now,
with its gardens of wisteria and gardenia
around the pool, and billiards room and
library and bedrooms for my children
and studies for my wife and me,
was once a dream home too.

Now my interests have diminished
while my children have grown and my dreams
that I built in stone have risen into a mist
finer than the fog of memory I've trailed while following
my dreams. That has always been the way with me,
this constant wiping out, this always starting over.
It's what keeps me close to the source.

Blumenthal's

Fifty-five years later and I can still smell the odor
of Tung-oiled wood and freshly dyed wool and
spools of thread. It smelled like a Chinese temple.

I'd go in there now and then, for mother,
to buy a few spools of red and black adjectives,
a shiny metaphor to snap things shut,
some nouns of bone. And, of course, silence.

The little bell above the door always jingled
delighted to see me, and the mahogany walls
of shelves and drawers darkened the air in there for me,

made a sanctuary for the sacred that I thought
could never be replaced. Until it was.
You know, the eternal thing that's holy in us
and changes from thing to thing to thing.

Dark Matter

I've lived my life as if I were my wife
packing for a trip—*I'll need this and that
and I can't possibly do without that!*

But now I'm about
what can be done without.
I just need a thin valise.

There's no place on earth
where I can't unpack in a flash
down to a final spark of consciousness.

No place where I can't enter
the joyless rapture
of almost remembering

I'll need this and *I'll need that,*
hoping to weigh less than silence,
lighter than light.

Here and There

We are so exposed in this life
we need pain to help guide us,
oxen to pull us and our heavy scenery
from here through the mists of sleep to there.

I love being here and there at once,
the mind's wake spreading its caravan
of dreams flowing over, under, and through me
to awaken miraculously back in this life.

I wonder if I've been touched
by grace to spend so much time
dwelling in the worlds I've imagined
are plunging through this one.

I wonder if others can unbuckle
the crushing gravity of the pronoun *me*
and love the pain of doing it in the then or there
whether they can do it or cannot.

Stone Koan

—for Michael Macklin

My student returns
and gives me a stone
as a parting gift.

It reminds me of you, he says,
showing me a side that's ribbed
like the shore at low tide
and a north face that looks like
something large has been sheered off.

It's a geode, he says.
Inside there's a cave
with sugar-white walls
and a city of glittering amethysts.

Part of me wants to crack it open.
Part of me does not.

Treasure Hunt

I felt like a stream rushing
over something shiny.
I couldn't tell what it was
I was constantly rushing
over but it was probably precious
because of that. Maybe it was
just a trick of light that kept me
diving for it my whole life.
I never told a soul about it.
It seems a lifetime ago. I was shining.
I can still make myself feel it.
I am the buried map.

Calling

You must realize
what I keep
bringing you
are separate pieces
of the same insight.

Carrying what
I can't express
from one darkness
into another
is a trade

so simple
the tools given me
are still nailed
where the walls
have fallen in.

Each day
is an empty house
with its one word
over my mouth
like a call.

Paradise

In a program called *Survivor Man*,
the host, after drifting five days at sea,
washes up in paradise: there's your coral reef,
the blue lagoon, and exotic colored birds
bouncing on palms in the balmy wind.

Later that day, he finds himself
under a pan-frying sun
among humongous cockroaches,
flesh-eating crabs, and fins
scissoring the island as if it were a cutout.

This paradise looks familiar, he thinks:
the woman he gave up everything for;
the career that turned into paperwork;
the crazy family life that left him hoping
for a quiet retirement.

So what is paradise? The longing to leave?
The leaving itself? In the end Survivor Man
tosses a message in a bottle out to sea.
It floats for years, then washes up in a place like this.

You Are What You Don't Eat

Finally one night my wife and I looked at each other
and said we're old. It took decades to admit this.
But we're young at heart and have made ourselves
go on a diet that requires we drink our weight in water
once a week to burn away what we don't want faster.

I had to get old to learn the hidden secrets of the aged,
that even straight-laced, pasty-faced Episcopalians think
stupid thoughts and continue to have sexual fantasies
like teenagers, but much more slowly as if they're tumbling
underwater. That's why they're quiet and smile a lot.

And we have to eat tiny little meals all day, like cows do,
and there's a lot of getting up and down instead of the jolts
of power walking. It's not that we need to lose weight.
It's the feeling that something in us is missing and it's growing
larger and we're disappearing and there's no time left to find it.

Lion Kings

I'm thinking that half-dead lion in the zoo
doesn't hear how loud his yawn is
any more than I do before my naps
when I relax and let my mind escape
like gas into the only luxury we aged have,
the cut-glass jewelry of forgetting ourselves.

That's where the violet sunset of otherness
air-brushes the scars and stiffened legs and broken teeth
we've lived with as if they were merely wisps
of consciousness being teased from our sleep.

The old lion's aches and pains seem pitiable.
But they are nature's kindnesses, an old wound
here and there, synapses that can't leap the gap,
an organ so barnacled with metastasizing cells
it's leaning toward collapse. But it's just Nature
slowly leading us by the hand to where the body
matters so little so far inside the blackness
we originally came from that it's magical.

Nature's saying you were here before
remembering, before one thing
became another, before your life
was the one deep breath you couldn't hold
any longer. Even the petals of a flower know that.
But the lion's yawn and mine are our way of
negotiating with the implacable. The deal is
if we leave here quietly and with a modicum
of dignity, we'll get to hear how loud we were
and how hard it was for us to enter.

Life on Earth

During my life on earth, I loved being
showered by the sun's colored protons
while seagulls screamed and days
dredged back and forth in the sexual smell of fish.

I loved my yellow consciousness
that was a long *yes* hovering above me
in blissful numbness like a gold ring
promised to a blue afterlife.

Yes, it was the sunlit numbness of being
in the moment that I miss, though I'm enjoying
the reverse: it all happening simultaneously,
and me, holding all of it inside me, totally dispersed.

Cloud, Backlit

6 a.m. March. Snow flurries.
I'm stepping into the Atlantic,
gulping fast, get-ready breaths
so I can swim furiously, numb
and red all over, to get out to my boat.

I practice my Zen training
which says if I utterly give in
to the cold, I won't feel how cold it is.

At dusk, I see a cloud backlit
so brilliantly it looks black
while the earth's atmosphere bathes it
in a perfume of pastel sherbet colors.

If my better half were here,
I would take this in without feeling
the need to tell about it
and making it all about myself.

This is the work I have to do, I tell myself.
Go ahead, I say, swim in it.
Force yourself if you have to.

II. Shell Game

I remember that I am falling
That I am the reason
And that my words are the garment of what I shall never be
Like the tucked sleeve of a one-armed boy

—W. S. Merwin, "When You Go Away"

Same Sea

The Adriatic off The Lido reminds me of the half-grubby Atlantic off of Winthrop where I grew up, except for the cabanas and posh hotels and teeming little sea creatures which I'm told Winthrop once had many years back. I could live here, I tell my wife, though I can't speak the language and couldn't get a job unless someone like me, only richer, who is as deeply interested in me as I have been, pays me to translate myself!

Once a loner realizes that it's the parade of ordinary people around him that makes him feel special, you'd think he'd no longer disdain the mundane for the ideal; which is why I thought Slovenia's pervasive polka music had a lot to do with its having the second-highest suicide rate in Europe. But, it turns out, no one speaks their language and its people, cupped at the bottom of the Julian Alps, feel like goldfish forever waiting for their water to be changed.

How can I get my feelings' colliding faces married to my knowledge? My India Air flight sat on the runway so long that I already knew I missed my connection before I ever departed. Even holding its broken wing in my lap, I would have ordered the captain to take off. Something in me just needed to feel there's a sea of difference between the Atlantic and the Adriatic, its littler self.

Walking gawkingly past a young nubile nude sunbathing in Piran, I say to myself, remember this: purple thong, the sky a Matisse blue, a ribbon of beige ambergris lacing the swells, the smell of roasted garlic and calamari, all of which I will take out now and then and rub, pleasuring my mind's thumb, like a smoothed down piece of polished sea glass. But, alas, wisdom, which comes neither waving a white handkerchief nor galvanizing itself in us with the force of a nude beauty, says that all women are my sisters. Knowledge says the sea glass is probably just a beer bottle somebody tossed.

My Life

was never large enough even for a B-movie
though I think I've felt as deeply as Brad Pitt.
No one I grew up with ever became famous
or notorious on that spit of land that ended in the sea.
But we became as adept at reading storm warnings
in the muscle and color of water as we did in a face.

In the cold-war doldrums of the 50's, all my teachers
hated teaching. We were such little shits back then
I thought who could blame them, and became a teacher
so I could show these younger versions of myself
how to open their hearts and enter into a different,
richer kind of darkness that exists in them.

We were an obstinate desert people given a single animal
which we rode and milked and roasted and skinned.
The stories strangers told us about fabulous places
we'd never get to taught us how to open a door in rock
and go inward, how to widen our hearts with longing
and a song and bang along on a drum skin and a string.

I think Mother and Father seemed larger than life because
we were smaller than them. That's how our life felt then,
heroic. Fate sat and watched from the empty bleachers
as surely as our shadows on the ground were having fun
parodying us. We didn't think making everything from
one thing was very special. We thought *we* were special,

and the day would come when some of us would finally
break through our smaller selves to prove it, and then
we'd have the luxury of looking over our shoulder
at a beginning we wouldn't want to return to any more
than Marilyn Monroe wanted to be Norma Jeane Mortenson
born in the charity ward of the L.A. County Hospital again.

When I think how far we've come and how epic our struggles
and how huge it feels to be alive, I wonder what it is in us
that needs to feel larger. Was it ever possible to be bigger
than ourselves? Something eternally young in me jumps up
and says *Of course it is!* But the teacher in me, the one who has
seen it all and looks like he hates teaching, says please sit down again.

Golden Watch

Teaching deep into the night
on my 65th birthday,
I found myself wishing
I could stop babbling on about
the mysteries of creativity
as if I could explain the art
of flight by hanging a stuffed owl
in a wind tunnel, forgetting
how I wished I could teach
back when my beard was black
and I had all the answers
and I was burning
to be respected for trying to
figure out who I was.

Well, now I'm longing to retire
from that wish because I know
enough about who I am
to relax and enjoy the way
the un-minded days
fall from my calendar
while I roll up the lint
of my loose ends into balls
I'll use as ear plugs
should the answers start to arrive again.

What will my empty days
be like, I ask myself?
But I'm not in.
I'm magnifying the head
of a fly to inspect its perspectives
on reality, magnifying its eye
the way my chest pains enlarge
my awe at all the little things
I missed because I spent
most of my life trying to be big.

Riding Shotgun in My Life

> *Victory: The sense that reality is more complete
> & perfect than the attainment of desire.*
> —Builders of the Adytum

Flying high over scrub brush blanketing the hills
like moss on rocks, I see a long scratch snaking
into the distance as if a kid trailed a stick that made
a dirt road into his future. Or maybe it's a riverbed.

I take a swig from some blue glacier melt
and wonder what happened to the child in me
who was obsessed with wandering the desert
when weekend nights after drunken fights

with my wife, who was always right, I'd toss
a shotgun in the trunk and blast west out of Texas,
past the praying, hard-as-rock mesquite trees
and lights thinning into a black absence

until my high wore off and I'd give up
and say, "Ok, go back. Apologize,"
remembering my therapist who told me suicide
was just my way of creating a new beginning.

That zealot in me, like the wilderness we cleared,
has disappeared. And the Dallas Metroplex is lit up
like a switchboard of tickled telephones.
Like America seen from space.

It feels like being happy may be heavier than
the years of wandering around inside myself hoping
for a fix from the voltage of epiphany.
But I have the world's worst memory.

And I know that this desolate landscape
and the old, desperate me are still inside me
and could rush up and swallow me
any time they choose if it weren't for

the control I've earned through all my mistakes.
But I don't even know why I seem to be happy,
much less know what's keeping this massive thing up.

Art

is the way a color says how
light feels: yellow for the
aerosol of happiness, black
for the zero of what isn't;
the way light, lined up right,
can cut through steel. Anything
is art if the mind's flawed right:
how soup feels being stirred,
how silence, broken open just so,
releases its essence and graces
the mind as a mint leaf in the air.

It's those who can't understand and
are dumbfounded by the obvious,
who thrive on dissonance and
subverting the ordinary into the
extraordinary who end up being
artists. What good is that, you ask?
No practical use as far as I can see.
In fact, Archimedes could've been
bragging about art's uselessness when
he said "Give me a long enough lever,
a place to stand, and I will lift the earth."

There is Nothing in My Hands

Tonight, after thirty years of teaching,
I weigh the puff of marble dust
my ten thousand steps have sanded off
against a sky that is true Popsicle blue.

They seem to weigh about the same to me.

Same way as tonight I'll read a great poem
and try to decide—
like all great magic tricks
whose fabulous physics unmask—
which is the truer of the two:
the secret life I've always wanted to lead
or the secret life I've led.

The Art of Living

I approached most things that needed my attention
in a hurry with a screwdriver and a hammer because
to be truthful I didn't care that much.

I was hurrying to equal the blur I was
trying to catch up to, to slow things down.
The tools were there to keep things in their place.

But sometimes, if I remember to whisper to myself
Make it happen, I can make an inner radiance
emanate out of me that dips everything in sparkles.

Then the old life that only came in black and white
with its thieving butchers and exhausted mothers
and angry ex-wives seems like some other poor bastard's life.

I must've "gotten over" something as we used to say
when a sickness had passed, or maybe my pride was hurt
since I'm not in a hurry to remember.

Just look at the scars on the faces of those tools.
Like a whole other kind of work. Like a climax in a movie.
For Chrissakes, they could be pieces of art.

Bucket Heads

33 years in The Academy
as a poet, a bit unbalanced
as if among the starched
scholars I had just swung
a haymaker at their silver-
tongued spritz of understated
arrogance and pungent smugness
and missed.

As an antidote, above my
posters of famous writers,
I keep a picture of Jake,
giggling and running
with a yellow bucket
for a hat on his head,
soggy Pampers between
his legs, and those shiny
patent leather shoes he'd wear
when he'd tap dance on
an extra door we put on the floor.

It's just a memory, a moment,
a magical grain of sand
staying the avalanche
of tacit disdain the tireless
scholars maintain for living
poets like me who they think
just play at their serious business
of learning and get what we want
whenever we want it out of the blue.

Catwalk, Flag Part, Tent Flap, Shoe Tongue

Yesterday in class
I was explaining how
metaphor works
when I looked down
and saw my fly was open.

Why, I asked my students,
wouldn't one of you tell me
I was unzipped
(which was, of course,
when everyone noticed)?

"I did this on purpose," I said,
"to demonstrate the power
of the controlling metaphor,"

and began plunging deeper
into the abstraction of absent-mindedness
by reciting several definitions
of the word "fly":
catwalk, flag part, tent flap, shoe tongue.

Cardinal Rules

> *You live only in the delirious illusion of language.*
> —Robert Penn Warren, "Brotherhood In Pain"

The male's easy to spot, red as a chili pepper
with his flamboyant crest and 2-note-c'mere-baby-whistle
scattershooting in all directions to attract some drab, young thing
who looks like she's been mixed in with the darks in the wash.

But that's not how he sees himself anymore than the ocean
thinks of itself as romantic. It's we who are guilty of sprinkling
the fairy dust of meaning on what we see, and end up feeling the way
our reflection on water liquefies into amoebic puzzle pieces.

Maybe that's why writing poetry never made sense to my father
who was fond of saying "That's how it is," and in the last years
of his retirement went grimly back to work as an airport screener
frisking thousands of people like himself for hidden explosives.

How many times did I turn red trying not to tell him, "I am
your-son-the-poet, the subversive with the explosives?
I am what I mean, and that's how it is," which, by the way,
if you ask me, is why the cardinal rules and is red.

Study: Imitation Long Grass with Nest

What kind of thing
would make its gray nest
in the middle of this
frozen explosion of long green
needles where the promise of birth
and home can't be gotten at
without being impaled?

The feeling of getting caught
red-handed comes to mind. Never mind
what I'm talking about—I'm talking about
the heart attack of it, the quill of guilt,
the slap and shock of being taken aback
by a green thing's scream.

But the absent bird that built the nest
seemed to say to me it's alright
to be who you are and where you're at,
and that out of this rain of upward arrows
something larger than new already in and beyond you
is being birthed will break through and fly
not then, not later, not other, not far. It says
you possess the magical power of empathy.
You're fine. It's yourself you're afraid of.

Shell Game

By remembering a beach 50 years ago,
the salty, dried-up smell of black seaweed
and crusted crab carapaces, the funky odor
of low tide pulling back over a pegboard
of muddy clam holes, I obliterate the present,

and remember the sapphire ring I got when I became a man
and lost on that beach, through whose jeweled, cobalt light
I loved to spy on what I desired, and by whose light
the whole world, as seen through the distances of my ignorance,
seemed as deep and beautiful as sleep.

*

I still haven't been able to realize the light
shining down on me whenever I lift my face comes from me,
that if I could just let go there'd be nothing left
to know, no point in knowing it, and no one, not even me,
having melted back into everything, to know about it.

And then there's you, dear reader, your remote control
about to slide the velvety blackness of an empty shell
over an inner life that's become a shrinking white pea
on a black screen, a pupil of light that says there's nothing
now or then, here or there, that does not see this.

.

B-Movie

I took the edges
of my experience
on two wheels
in bad weather
letting other people
I pretended to be
drive through the lashing
rain. What a waste
I must've looked like:
good kid gone bad,
two-bit hood
going in circles
in a stolen ride.
Like Paul Newman
racing and making
salad dressing
and giving it all
away. Except I'm smaller
and more anonymous,
like you, my friend, starring
in your own *film noir* cameo,
replete with pigeons
frightening the air
under the almost human
scream of the El
shadowed by people
in slouched hats
and trench coats
smoking inside you.
No one plays it safe.
Not even if you're belted in
and glommed onto the TV,
you're on the edge,
owning nothing, leaning
into the screeching
curves, sinking deeper into
the edges of the moment,
learning how to love things
slowing down as you go

faster and the colors
saturate you as you
get larger than life
going nowhere fast
with me beside you
screaming these are
our salad days
as you turn toward
the camera and smile.

One Last Wish

If I were given the chance to live my life over,
I realize everything I'd change would shrink
in comparison to having to erase my parents.
It's not so much that it would smudge me back
into abstraction, it's more that shadowy sense
of never being able to land anywhere solid.

There's nothing in the world I'd rather be born from
except what I can't change. That's my prime directive,
like on Star Trek, "Don't interfere," as I plunge deeper
into the wheeling star field which turns out to be a succession
of lost opportunities and mistakes I made and blew past
in favor of feeling I was getting somewhere. Well,

that never ends. So I look forward to passing into blackness
but with the feeling of moving still there. Black fires everywhere.
The fear-quills of my self-consciousness finally fallen off.
Why go back and live another life when I'm just about there?
I wish I had the power of not looking back. Not the power of having
a wish granted, but the power to look at my wish and see behind it.

Extracting the Essence

My brother's retired under the Florida sun
with no place to be, no one to see, and no job
to be done. He smokes his cigar beside the pool
whose unreal blue circles and blurs and subdues
the distant hum of rush-hour traffic into liquid bliss.

I wonder, picking the glint off the briars of silence
between us, why doesn't my brother want to be wakened
from all these years of doing nothing, but I hold my breath,
say nothing in the way he drove relentlessly toward success
just so he could stop and make this silence a gift to himself
as rich as what his wealth has brought him.

I'm reminded of his scientific work, which was to extract
the basic flavor from foods and recreate it chemically
so the world could have a cuisine as lean and illusory
as the molecular essence of American happiness.
I am just a poet watching the aromatic steam rise
from the evanescent chemistry of quiet between us,

which I'm recreating into my own table of elements,
an alphabet that makes something beyond meaning,
like mother, gone now 20 years, calling us to supper,
putting down steaming food on the table between us
so we could grow up and get out. And what about father,
whose life with four volatile kids took a hard left turn
with maintaining his snappy sense of Las Vegas romance.
I don't remember him saying much.

Nose Job

—for Jessie

My daughter calls and says she wants a nose job.
You got a lovely nose, I say. I like your little speed bump.
On Father's Night at school she warns me, Dad, don't do anything
crazy. Could she be referring to the time I stuffed raisins up my nose
and blew them into my lasagna? Or the time when we wrestled
and I secretly smeared bloody ketchup on my face? Or the time I stuffed
a kiwi under my arm and asked if anyone knew about cancer?

I wonder what the cost of this, her latest path to happiness, is,
but I take the high road and say, Darling, in our inmost self
we have no face. Oh Dad, she says, no one thinks like that.
So I tell her both my sisters who had nose jobs ended up
divorced and lonely. But then I come clean and admit that
all my fantasies have been of *shiksa* types who look like
ads for rhinoplasty, that I would've chosen another nose too
if I could've, something polished and chiseled and noble,
not this thing that passes for a party honker.

I tell her about the Buddha who met a man and instantly
killed him because the Buddha knew this man would
slaughter millions. I tell her the story of how I fell in love
with a gentile from New Hampshire, how once her blue-blood folks
got a load of my nose they sent me packing broken-hearted
and defeated. But, the bottom line is this, my darling daughter:
if it weren't for this nose you curse and dismiss, which must be
part of what your mother fell in love with, you wouldn't exist.

Human Flames

Jake, telling your mother *Screw you!*
then running off to a girlfriend
who's holding on to you
just to forget who she is
is just another way of our being
beautiful, slow-burning flames
giving back everything we are
to where we came from,
which you're doing perfectly.

I remember sitting inside
the house I built of failure
for over twenty years
until, adjusting to what
I keenly believed in,
like a Tibetan monk I finally saw
that what I was doing was right
by the light my body threw off.

Jake, I'm holding my life up to you
as once, when nothing could console you,
I took you outside and held you up
to the light of the full moon
so you could hear the vast darkness
saying I'm lost too, to say that most of what I prize
has been used up or broken, and because of that
it's more beautiful and true; and
to tell you the truth that I'm still lost,
more prodigal than you.

Wild Onions

Like the break in a game of 8-ball,
my son, the student-pharmacist,
dreams of molecules busting up
under the Bunsen burner's alchemical
blue flame, its steadfast faith in being
on fire, conjuring up smoke and bubbles.

In the antiseptic, white fluorescence
of the franchise pharmacy, I hand the clerk
a prescription for my nitroglycerin, confident
it will blow my arteries open when I need
to extract the pick-axe from my chest.

The row of pharmacists, bent over,
counting, have vowed obliviousness
to the sick who've jumped through loops
of the telephone tree to stutter out
the chemical abracadabras that will
scour away the barnacles of aging.

When he was little my son announced
his plan to live for free in a cardboard box
behind the All-You-Can-Eat steak restaurant.
Not much different from wanting to be a druggist
on the graveyard shift, I thought. Anonymous
as the face of a pill. No one to bother him.

But what about his passion and vivacity
of mind, I ask my wife? Don't you see,
she says, he's chosen to be your opposite.
You've poured everything you are into
what you do and nothing else. All the rest
who live in the world live in that nothing else.

Just before my father died he asked—
and he wasn't fishing for a compliment—
how'd he have such smart kids? He couldn't
explain it any more than I could make him
understand my wanting to be a poet. At least
part of it comes from you, I said, and he took that in
reluctantly, like a bitter antidote to his jagged
looking backward over a rugged life.

Come to think of it, I did the opposite too.
Wasn't I the wild onion in his garden of kids?
And before I go I'm hoping to see the upside
of my regrets. That would be my offspring
who in their turn are determined to grasp
their freedom by doing everything the opposite.

Mariscos

—for Allison Hedge Coke

I thought I was doing my job
"fulfilling my purpose
on this earth," as they say,
the way every creature
from ant to amphibian
goes about its business
in headlong allegiance
to a prime directive
that says work is faith,
and lacks the defeatist
questioning with which
some little lost part of me
won't stop interviewing
the larger part of me that's lost,

when I sat down to a bowl of
mariscos del mar, whose
mollusk and shellfish sat glumly
sunk in a primordial broth,
with a Native American poet
who called me her mentor,
whose blandishments in life,
she laughingly explained,
have been one long horror show
after another, from rape to abuse
to diaspora, and who talked about
helping the poor in this world
who don't have water or work
and can't defend themselves
against the greed and corruption
of murderous governments,

and felt my sense of purpose
thin to the razor I'd been
shaving off slices of my life with,
as if I had eaten the whole cow
by slivering it into transparent

flitches of carpaccio smothered
in virgin olive oil and lemon
and topped off with spicy capers
for the pleasure of the gourmand
Italian thug in me to eat,

as she kept beaming
and offered to take me
to the *barrios* of Columbia
to read my poems to people
who were dying from a lack of
spiritual encouragement, read
about my suburban doings
that began to look to me like
the foulard of orange grease spots
floating on top of my tepid soup.

I felt my heart enlarge inside
the emptiness that asked
if there'd be an honorarium
and wasn't a war going on down there
and would it be safe for someone like me
who's living out, no, floating on top of,
no, spilling out of the American Dream?

Sometimes in this life an angel
appears in a disguise we can't imagine,
maybe as a student who looks
beyond the blackness drowning us
in muck where, in the difficult light
of hearing who we're supposed to be,
a purpose finds us that will feed us,
makes us stand up from bottom-feeding
on the exotic and expensive and,
with that clarifying sense of emptiness
reverberating in our hearts, fortifies us
with enough to enter the obliterating world.

In

I've been sailing my boat
in the tub, refusing to get out,
until I can navigate the tumultuous

geographies of my inner Americas,
arts as beautiful and riotous as a child's
questioning, quills of sub- and hyper-
frequencies whistling by my perception.

Would it be too untoward to ask,
at my age, what's been taken away to make me
so selfish and little that I prefer

to endure the preternatural bellowing
of the foghorn vibrating the ship I'm in
to the dead calm glumly containing it?

While I was waiting to be chosen, waiting chose me.
So I slapped an alphabet on a Rubik's cube
and twisted it until the colors matched

where I thought I was at, which is to say,
in the end it looked like when I started.
Normally this would be the place in the story

where the hero plunges the buoy of his heart
into some godforsaken trackless patch of space
and has a gymnasium named after him.

So I plunge into myself and from there
try to catch up with where I'm sailing.
The heroic part is in the enormity of what

we consider normal: on a small blue planet
at the tail-end of a galaxy in a foaming cluster
of gazillions of other galaxies, a small soul
is trying to master sailing a tub in a boat.

Stupid Human Tricks

I dreamt all night of different ways to kill the President
but I kept getting caught. I guess my days are
so compressed by the real world I don't get a chance
to really spin out aside from writing about what I haven't done.
Speaking of fantastic work, how about that guy
who wrote the Bhagavad-Gita on his toenails?
Where'd he get such a tiny pen?

I probably have a higher purpose too
but I never knew what that meant. Something bigger
than me and heavier than accomplishment
but not the knockout of epiphany? My little *shih tzu*
who loves to sleep has been genetically wired
by centuries of Chinese emperors to warm my feet.
That makes me, pathetically, his higher purpose.

I've jerry-rigged myself to look peripherally
for the shadow of meaning, meaning usually
I miss the obvious. It took me years to figure out
when my dog licks his lips he means it's time to eat.
Now that was an epiphany. I do it right back at him
when I feel wicked, the way God does to me when
once in a blue moon he thinks I should believe in him.

Mean Streak

The last time I visited my old Hebrew School,
weeds had broken through and crumbled
the asphalt back into its original, Biblical black dirt.
And the ornate, heavy iron fence I once imagined
were rows of Centurion spears must've been
sold by the ton and melted down for scrap.

All of us soon-to-be-barmitzvahed boys heaped
curses on that place, hoping it would end like this.
Just as certain bastards in the past who hated me
have died, which a part of me I'm not proud of likes
to take credit for. Just keep it up, I'd think, and

I promise to unleash by some mystical indirection
I intuit an unlucky end for you. And when they kept
it up, my feelings secretly went to work on them.

How wondrous having evolved from being a reptile
into a bird. And a singing bird at that.
But still just a bird.

So you see, I'm not the man I'd like to think I am.
I'll end up being weird like my uncles and aunts
whose rubbery caricatures of gargoyles and beasts
I have become and have come to respect, because
in the face of all they weren't—urbane, accomplished,
cool, and spiritual—they were at least themselves.

Unstable

All along he had the feeling his life was a voice-over
narrated to him by a third party, so he always worried
about what the audience thought.

His favorite food, lobster, was another thing
he had brought up into the light and air
and boiled in its own element.

Meanwhile, elsewhere, fabulous extensions
of the senses were being invented by his peers:
eyes spinning light years into deep space, ears
that could taste the charms and flavors in an atom.

All this while thrusting his mind inside itself
to say what he was feeling, hoping, like a child
locking his double-jointed legs around his neck,
this trick was bigger than it was. And it was

in the sense that he turned not understanding
into an art for the anonymous few throwbacks who shared
a similar malady while the movers and shakers of the world
played craps with electronic signals and facts.

Oh, well, he thought, could this be the wrong world
again, checking the map in his mind he made
as a child that showed everywhere he wasn't.
Which, of course, it was. Which, of course, it wasn't.

Intimacies of Cleaning

They have wiped off what I said
from my keyboard, sprayed the splatters
of toothpaste, and shaken out the arabesques
of beard and pubic hair into the trash.

What do I know of them? They stop talking
in Spanish when I enter the room.

I know Sonya's grandson, the first
in the family to go to college, was shot
dead in an argument over his girlfriend,
that all her revolving helpers are illegals,
and her mother's dying in Guanajuato because
that's what she said when she couldn't come.

What does she know of me?

That I don't sleep so well and my heart's
not right, that I'm taking antidepressants
because she rearranges my pills. I overhear her say
I'm falling apart so fast I won't make it to my death.

I know she sneaks extra strips of twist-ties
out of the house but leaves the loose change
from the couch out where I can see it.
That her trailer is crowded with relatives
from Mexico, she says, who won't ever leave
or get off their butts to help out.

I pay her in cash and she pretends we know nothing
of each other's lives, that she's not there when she cleans.
But why, after she dusts every photo and picture in the house,
does she leave all of them crooked? I don't want to know.
I answer the door and tell her where to start cleaning,
abajo or *arriba* according to where I won't be at.

Fragments

> *You are that awareness, disguised as a person.*
> —Eckhart Tolle

I am back to crawling over everyone
to get back to who I am, back to that stillness.

Each of us is a missing fragment of the other
which creates the cave-in blocking our way.

I look around in the dark for the way and see
it's a Pointillist painting I can't stand back from.

The same with purity which is not a long inhalation
on nothingness but is paying attention to everything.

It's no good focusing on whatever comes next. The sign on
Razzmatazz's Crab Shack promises "Free crabs tomorrow!"

What good is having all the tools you need
if your life feels like a dream you had in another life?

What good's an eternity of trial and error
if the sum of all our fragments is something more than us?

Tomorrow a dragonfly will land inches from my face.
I will look huge in his glistening Beluga eyes.

We'll stare at each other long enough to stop time
which is what it takes to bring me back to myself again.

Any Minute Now

Without knowing it, all along
I have been adding things up,
savoring faces, holding grudges,
exploring the intricate knots
in what happened in the belief
that after all the laborious clambering
and the confusion of understanding
everyone's point of view, I half-expect
to break out of myself and reach
some resolving, epiphanic Scenic View

where without knowing it
I'll see, after all, yes, something
larger but much more subtle's been at work,
keeping me balanced, even as
the earth turns at 1,000 mph
and my son stares up helpless
at the balloon he's let go of
and I think *shit* but promise
it's going to the moon.
It's not enough to be wise.

Helpmeet

I used to live at the speed
of an elastic snapping back
to where I was originally at.
Some new misunderstanding.

But you can't blame people for yearning
to climb a great idea. Like some wise man
who also found the world to be difficult
once said if the mountain were smooth
you couldn't climb it.

Inside us there's a path across which
a rockslide of mistakes has crashed,
a cargo of stones you could pile into
a monument to honor what you lacked
if you stood on a mountain of humility to do that.

Still Smoldering

The fire's still there. Maybe it's not
the sprigs of wildfire I once doused
in a gasoline of dreams but it's still there,
shimmering reddish-orange under a blanket
of whatever I burned off getting here

along with the charred stumps of not doing
what I was told. So if I look concussed,
staggering off, please consider that my heart,
which had me try on everything I wasn't,
and made me feel like a stranger to my self,
which made me understand who I am, is quiet.

Is it me that's lit from within? Everything seems it is:
human flowers blooming inside gridlock traffic,
children playing hide-and-seek in old people's faces,
the soul's purple anesthesia expanding until
it's your own aura, a smile inside the nothing

in particular of being here as half-smoke, secret glitter,
standing stunned before pyramids of fruit inside
the local Tom Thumb's. Outside it is winter. Clouds
are spinning down pure white intricately etched ashes
of what will again be water, whether the fire's still there or not.

III. Beggar's Cup

Nothingness carries being in its heart.

—Jean Paul Sartre, *Being and Nothingness*

Past Due

Though we grew up poor at the edge of the sea,
blizzards of snow, hurricanes, and floods
were luscious fruit thrown at us. Nothing
was more exciting than to be sent out to play
in what grownups worried about. A day off
from school opened our hearts like flowers
from The Gigantic Period. We were the prize
in a Cracker Jack box. If the world wasn't
wonderful to the grownups who were immigrants
in our world, then all the wonder must've been in us.

Long story short, I was little and skinny and no good
at breaking rocks, my teachers said. And for crimes
I have no memory of, they sentenced me to be
bewildered all my life. So who's going to invite me
to public school to speak? But it's the little gods
in the guise of the kids who are dangerous. Thank God
we can throw them across the room, the grownups said.
Thank God they can't escape from their crazy bodies.
Thank God we're grownups. But it doesn't just happen
by growing old. First you have to grow up and get over
yourself. Then, if you get to be as old as us, you'll forget
everything except you'll remember you paid your dues.

Birth Day Party

Memory in her drab gray dress was the first to arrive.
She sat there bored, with nothing to remember,
so she talked to herself, her mind streaming
like a black-and-white tickertape of words.

Upstairs, Regret circled and circled her mouth
in hard red, ironed the wrinkles out of an old
embarrassment, and doused herself in lavender.

Beaten off from humping Memory's leg, Happy
rolled over and over, his little thoughts
like the insides of a Scrabble box.

Hard Work trudged downstairs
to the basement to soak and snooze
in the anesthetizing glow of the cathode tube.

Part of me was there too. The omniscient narrator.
A *you* without a mouth. A mist of a face
in a black-on-black painting.

The rest of me, never having tasted or seen
or heard or been held before, was about to arrive.
Everyone cried and was glad somebody had the chance
at being someone again. That was the occasion.

Going Away Party

> *Inside every old person is a young person*
> *asking "How the hell did this happen!?"*
> —sign inside some old person's bathroom

I deftly second-guess and sidestep the antagonist's
certain downfall. I improve on a superhero's power
so now he can transform into anything. Then I turn the TV off
to attend a going-away party for octogenarians.

I find it hard to look at the old man with a cotton wad
sticking out of his left nostril. Does he even know it's there?
Maybe he doesn't give a damn anymore. The live jazz trio
has closed its eyes and sinks deeper inside its muzak.

My wife insinuates I'm having trouble growing old.
I say not so but I feel like I'm stuck at a hideous petting zoo.
One of the beasts with a half-lamb, half-human face, lectures me
with a mouthful of coleslaw on women's suffrage.

Back home my wife says, "Isn't it wonderful how their minds
are still sharp!?" But I've already caught the tail end of a thriller
in which there's only a few seconds left before all humanity
will become extinct if I can't figure out which wire to cut.

Someone Else's Shoes

I found them one night after last call on a bench by the river,
as if they had finally had enough, would go no farther,
just wanted to sit there while their sorry owner walked home
drunk that winter night, wet socks and all, to apologize to his wife.

They fit as if they belonged to a guy who was bigger than me,
the way sometimes I'll smoke a cigarette and catch myself
wishing I were smoking a cigarette, the way sometimes I feel
there's a life inside this life I'm leading that I'm not living.

So, I've walked in someone else's shoes, but I'm not better for it.
The guy who left them probably said, "Wait here, I'll be back
in a minute," and then, like a *penitente* whipping himself with guilt,
went home barefoot over ice and snow to beg his wife's forgiveness,
which is when I came by.

Home

Gloves that have done years of work,
been left in the dirt, rained on, dried out,
and broken in again have become molds
of the hands that remade the world and turned it

into us. What we long for when we're away
from home is whatever will receive us as we are
in the mute world of things and speaks of us
so soothingly we luxuriate in the cliché of a long *ahhhh*.

We say it's good to be home. But we have forgotten
who we are, that the thing in us that's restless, always
slipping over the distant edge of where and what we are,
cannot leave its imprint on anything that is, but is.

Paean against Pain

I praise the pill that pinpricks my waking
and countersinks me like a headless nail.

I praise the gas whose molecules carry off
every dot of my pixilated consciousness.

I praise the colorless IV that rushes me
into transparency, the anesthesiologist

placing the delicate aroma of who I am
inside a bubble of water, where my mind is

snowing and my body's burning
in the cold light of another world

that weighs less than everything I am.
Let us praise the gap, the shunt, the disconnect

that blocks, switches, smothers, or numbs
the alarm of ourselves going off. Let us praise

ourselves who may not have created us
but from us invented the *is* that is not.

In the Dark

—In memoriam: for my son Jacob Myers, 1985-2009

Anger and sorrow have split off from me
like twin tree trunks. I think I will grow in
opposite directions like this from now on,
watching the fruit of what I can hardly bear open.

When I dared to look at my son's ashes,
I said "focus," but I could not accept that this
was what's left of my boy who, just yesterday,
freshened the world with his jasmine presence.

I would've jumped in front of the bullet, I would've
killed for him, but he was the one who took his life
leaving me swirling in mid-air while the world emptied
itself out and became more meaningless and precious.

I am struck dumb, twisted inward, and folded over
by something so final that I have sworn to stay alive
just to spite death, just so I can stick a thumb in its eye
and then follow through looking for my son in the dark.

Eating Grief

The wind cups a few sparks of fear
carefully so as not to blow them out.

Sadness lifts its head like a horse in darkness.
My beloved son is dead and I walk backward,

lowering The End like a rock curtain,
tasting metal in the silence that attaches itself

to the electrodes of memory. Flashbacks of Jake
scorch the surface while my feet can't touch bottom.

Mind-howls spread and even themselves out
among the smithereens of wind and light.

I am blinded by the guilt that gold-rims my thoughts
like a set of bone china which I am given to eat grief from,

a kind of mouth-to-mouth resuscitation to bring him back
to life. I passed on to my son the opposite of every mistake

I ever made, crushing him between propriety and homilies.
Tonight dew drops jewel the leaves and the clouds air-brush

the moon as if beauty were brain-dead to the sky
curling like a burning photo. Each day is a fresh grave

dug into me. Everything I do is instilled with the care
of the frail and aged. As my spiritual beliefs slide away

from what is, every thing is becoming a holy remnant.
My son's death is deathless and backlights the world.

Renovation

You slid out from under your ironic smile
and collapsed everything. Now the renovations
of memory, in a whine and slog of hammers and saws,
dust the present's onrushing transparencies
with the small swirlings of forgettings.

That's how I can cook an egg or take a walk
out of loss's tar pit. Why my wanting to crush
everything into an unrecognizable mass is now
balanced by the fluttering of a moth. It's not
denying death that feels surreal. It's what's real.

I could've been a tank commander in a former life
the way I keep imagining locking onto beauty
and exploding it. Then how fresh an average day smells,
as if opening the hatch your punishing absence were over.
As if the miraculous were ordinary. As if you came home.

Wall of Absence

For a moment I wasn't obsessing about you
being gone. You were truly gone.
Then the heart-pangs began because I didn't want
you to have been so alone when the walls swallowed you.
Half-crazed, I thought if I could become transparent
then maybe I could reach you.

But I'm just an old man holding onto some curled-up snippets
on the cutting room floor of your all too brief life—Jake,
you didn't make the clean getaway you thought you could.
Look back at us left devastated, disbelieving and blinking
in the blue-black after-image of your life.

I never told you this, but I remember the exact moment
I conceived you, how I thrust all that was good in me,
like a pink storm of storks taking off and blurring into the eternal,
into who you'd become. But I forgot that all of the dark
matter that also made me would eventually undo you, bring us
to this dead-fall wall of absence each day is.

Neither Here nor There

We are "star stuff contemplating star stuff,"
Carl Sagan said, having risen up
into a voluminous cosmic awareness
to point to the fiery origins of our consciousness.

I once thrilled to that great evolutionary journey
from the stars to a destiny within. Yet
as I look at my poor son's ashes
I can't make myself believe that's him,

couldn't make myself scatter his ashes
in the desert, can't let go his holy remnants.
What I'm left with is an angry, shrunken God
and an infinite number of planes of existence
I can't see they say are shooting through me.

And yet my son is everywhere. In the shock
of a kid's brown hair, in the adolescent slouch
of a smoking silhouette, and the dented anvil
remembering the hammer, the hammer ringing

while I try on the same old life that's too small,
too big, too short, too long, living badly
in two places at once, neither here nor there.

To-Do List

Do nothing.
Be the dot in the center.
The hole without a thought.
Move like the globules
in a lava lamp.

Let others burn in the whiteout
of ideas, the blackout of action.
Let the vanishing point inhale
me and my consciousness and the whole
landslide of mistakes and lost chances
behind my closed eyes.

Usually and mostly

I feel like sleeping now,
drifting off into a pixilated numbness
in which my own idiosyncratic symbols
of failure have starring roles in my dreams.

Usually they're about something I can't do
or where I should've been, and, of course,
the faceless woman I'm trying to find my way back to.

The harder I try to make something inside believe me,
the longer the woman has no face.

Usually the dreams end with me collapsed
against something frozen open or rusted shut,
and I wake feeling all tangled up and think,
That was weird . . . Then I go through the day
like a jet flying through a cloud bank,
a cloud bank sensing there's a needle in it,
unsure, though, the way this poem's not sure
it's a poem.

The World's Highest Mountain

My little poems are wind-whipped lean-tos,
like prayer flags studding the Himalayas.
I sit inside, make a fire, brew some leaves,
and arrive at where I've always been.

Outside, a snowstorm of questions blows across
frozen answers, as if the world were an empty cenotaph.
We are all our own holy cenotaphs: the one who made
a poem or built a house or ascended what he thought

could be done and then went on to plant his flag
in eternity. In the end if the work each one has done
has made a space inside for someone else, it's sacred.

When the Angel Came for Him

he began a poem
about his life
and those who
brought him here
and how he grew up
and the ocean he loved
gliding through
and the women he met
who vanished
into a beautiful smoothness
until a book was done
and more and more flashes
from a previous life
and the one beyond this one
came to him and it was
limitless this making art
of the life he'd led,
having failed in making
an art of living it.

So as the Angel
watched his desperation
sweat like gold,
she revealed to him
it's all the same to her
whether all this takes
a second, an eternity,
or another life, his life
was just a flickering
of who he is, and that
beyond himself, burning
clear as the sun beyond
both night and day,
however he lives
it's the living
that makes an art of it.

Beggar's Cup

I'm slowing down now,
imperceptibly, it seems,
like a river spreading itself out into a delta
where the minute metallic taste of salt, like paradox
blooming in the darkness, takes me out.

I can see down the road that someday soon
I'll give in to this and with one deep breath
dissolve as easily as the memory of splashing headfirst
into this life has drifted invisibly beyond feeling.

*Old age always arrives with his two companions:
sickness and regret,* an old woman says to me.
Then come the war stories wearying as her pain
which she feels is front-page news to me
but is only the door to after she exists.

Now, before my ego breaks down
into a pile of pick-up sticks,
before my final dispersal rolls in on the swell
of some never-before-felt feeling that releases me,
I'm wondering where my consciousness will go,

if after death I'll still be a me, minus the striving
and million forms of the fear of dying
that's misshapen whatever is left of me
because I was so deeply living it.

Time to sink back into the world again
which, like a colony of panicky ants, continues
to dismantle and carry off bit by bit
the fragile sense of unity I once glimpsed of it.

Here, I say, with my empty beggar's cup,
to anyone who will listen, is what I was able to fill up.
It's the joy of simply being. Which took my whole life to make.
It contains all that's left behind of me and when I'm gone,
everything I am. And it'll stand for everything I wasn't.

The Amnesiac's Memoir

I no longer feel guilty about not being able to recall
much at all, but have come to think of it as an honor
I've earned on my way to perfecting my development.

If I rent the same movie day after day and don't
realize I've seen it until I find myself lip-syncing
with Clint Eastwood: "*Deserve* has nothing to do with it,"

the lapse makes my senior moments seem more exotic,
the way driving off and forgetting where I'm going,
come to think of it, makes the world newly abnormal.

I remember when I was little, hearing the scary old ragman
calling for clothes that would be stripped of their history
to make the finest paper. Like them, I have been chosen to ascend

and join myself in forgetting everything I've ever been through
in the hope that soon I will be blank and gleaming and pour
into the life-long white potential I sensed in my beginning,
which, apparently, ever since I've been pouring through.

The Golden Years

Things are beginning to soften
and blur back into what they were.
I seem to be listening from inside
a golden mask, a mild narcosis,
ceremonially being lifted up
atop the wave of the living moment
and guided toward erasure.

Someone from a great distance
is prepping me to ask a question
either he forgot or thought better of.
Meanwhile the young fast-forward
through me like sharp objects,
like my aches and pains and flashes
squabbling for attention.

Which reminds me of a story I can't resist
spreading out like crumbs of wisdom
before my pigeons, my brethren, who look up
at me warily with one eye on the sky,
no longer able to turn wild at a moment's notice.

I'm what a gorgeous diamond engagement ring
feels like shining inside its black velvet box.
Such a small space in which to be married
to vastness, swooning into less and less.
To have and to hold and to keep.

What the Old Master Said

—for Jack Gilbert

Before he left, the old master spoke of his failing memory,
about being embarrassed over feeling so young while looking old,
about his misgivings over a life lived so severely that his normalcy
seemed egregious. It allowed him I think to see clearly over
great distances albeit mostly into the past. But now and then,
looking me in the eye, he would continue the conversation
we were having beneath our conversation, which was about two old men
agreeing there's no difference between them, how there's nothing more
important beyond sharing the spirit. I never heard from him after that.

Cholangiocarcinoma

Here in the oncology ward, bald and nauseous,
we wait for the intercom to call our turn
under the red buzz of the radiation gun
or the chemo bag that's slowly dripping
as if something above us were melting.

Everyone's faced the fear of leaving the world
at one time or another, but the alien world
of cells blooming into barnacles inside us, then
into coral reefs that'll one day unexpectedly
detonate makes death seem like a welcome blackout.

Anupa, a beautiful Indian techie in purple, butterflies
among the despondent as if she were what is possible.
Have I ever gone through the world feeling beautiful?
Maybe when I was tumbling underwater and everything
wanted to touch me. My memory can just barely feel that.

That was when I was as wildly thriving as what's broken off
and gone crazy in us. I miss those heady times. And I'll miss
the time when they'll have shrunk cancer back down into
a word like *dyspepsia* and there'll be a pill for it. Meanwhile
my eyes have turned yellow. I need a liver immediately.

That seems to have made the knowledge of death quicken
something in me that's ripened into the exquisite kind of
sweetness you see in little children and the gently senile.
Everything has been planned for me down to the last minute.
I'm waiting as fast as I can for a stranger's fatal accident.

Every Thing

The only liver fluke I ever saw
was in Junior High biology lab
which bored me. It looked like
a gray, deflated football, and I said
Yuk, and dutifully drew a picture of it
next to my splotch of Jello-y amoeba
not having the slightest inkling
it'd be a fluke that'd eventually
come to kill me.

I love weird, unlucky stuff like this
where the hero's running out of time
trying to figure out how he got poisoned
by an Asian liver fluke, which restaurant—
the Double Happiness, Thai One On, or
the Lover's Wok—he ate his mussels in,
until he figures out that's not what matters.

My little liver fluke only wants
what I want, to be smothered in
gardenias and have his spirit blossom
into a gorgeous cholangiocarcinoma,
rivers jammed with flowers that want their seeds
to snow like golden flakes in a twirling tarantella
on which the universe grows huge, consuming itself.

One doesn't have to be a poet to be a poet.
Everything, by merely being, is in profusion,
and in profusion, there's joy. It's a riot of everything
wanting to turn everything else into itself.
Merely by being, by having once been,
it has not left itself behind.

American Bardo

When I looked death in the eye
and it said it's just oxygen,
breathe deep, I studied
that moment's dimensions
as if I had taken a face,
any face, say my face,
and put it on the big screen
where just because of its size
and the fact that every face
is one of a kind, amazing
if you really look at it,
it made the masked face of the anesthesiologist
look galvanized up there in the distance
like a tiny music, and I forgot
all the hard work it took for me
to settle things with death,
to say, ok, I'm ready, instead of
me fading away, spinning around,
going down backwards like a bug
flushed away in the big moment
while everything in me felt like
I was a radio blaring without its speaker,
and there was no time, no depth,
like an airplane flying between
two sheets of glass, and then this voice
with fingers snapping inside it
when I was crossing over and wasn't sure
where I was, what plane I was on,
just this flat voice saying "Wake up, it's over."

Grave Question

My wife says she's made up her mind
she wants to be cremated. Perhaps, the shrink
in me thinks, it's because she was thrown out
of the house when she was a kid. Didn't I want
to be cremated every minute I was kid? Anyway,
she says what's it matter when you're dead.

So why am I reduced to eenie, meenie,
minee, moe-ing over a grave or an urn?
No one in my hometown remembers me,
and the vicissitudes (which should be
a major book in the Bible) have blown away
my kids as if I were a dandelion gone to seed.

I think I'd feel comfortable with cremation
if there were a picture of me on the urn.
Hmmm, so my vanity has made the dilemma
say uncle, though if I were being *flambéd*,
I'm sure my pride wouldn't be one of the
vital essences steaming from my brain.

But being buried I'd have the chance to write
my epitaph, give those who visit a minute
to ponder the meaning of life, or make light
of man's highest achievement, the predicament
of being conscious of the end. Or I could make something
beautiful. But I tried doing all that when I wasn't dead.

No, death deserves something more special. After all,
it's bigger than a birthday. Maybe I should give myself
back to whence I came, just limp off into the woods
like an animal and melt into the universe. I've never
seen a bird drop from a tree. And disappearing has
dignity and mystery, not to mention a memorial service.

Then there's cryogenics and pyramids and burial at sea.
Perhaps I could get the best of both worlds by being
only partially buried and leaving my head for the urn.
At any rate it's obvious I'll have to dig deeper into who I am
in order to find out how to get rid of me.

String Theory

Let me see if I get this right . . .
On different planes there are
an infinite number of me's
living out all my possibilities
in a life of their own without me.

While I believe everyone's unique,
just like everyone else, something in me
feels infinite, though I worry if I were
me in another life wouldn't I feel like
the same as me in this life?

It's comforting to picture little me's
being everywhere at once, popping
like popcorn kernels into something larger,
feeling good knowing that somewhere else
I've finally fulfilled my promise.

This

I should have made a temple out of my study.
But I studded it with accomplishments
and walled it in with books I nodded over
like a pilgrim at the Wailing Wall.

I knew when I was doing this,
that someday I'd regret
making who I was
into something I had done.

I knew there'd come a time when this lifetime
of mistakes would be just scattered atoms
in the earth's unconsciousness.

But I couldn't wait to be more than what I was,
and I took that atom and blew it up
into self-aggrandizement and went ballooning
so I could show the world what I could do
which showed the world what I had done.

Plans

I thought of my soul as something like a scent,
like an air of kindliness. That my selfish heart
would grow enormous in battle. I thought I could help
the troubled because I was troubled. I wanted my humility
to be large, to float like a balloon above the parade I was in.

But you know how it goes. My epic turned out to be
a miniature self-portrait painted on a brick from a wall
in me that had fallen in. My oxen were small as bugs.
My arrows that I imagined shredding the sky like black rain
in a Japanese ink print melted back into brushstrokes.

So it's good to feel small once more, to bow at the end
of a long line of becoming everything again. No more
struggling to fit in after wind-light sweeps me up or a dying
ember takes me in as easily as I thought my life should have been.

Or maybe what's next will be harder or nothing or I'll be
totally surprised without there being a me. I always felt like
that anyway. But the place in me where all of this is missing
has turned sacred over time. That's the best explanation I have
for why we aren't allowed to know even the simplest things.

Desert is the Memory of Water

After I am gone and the ache begins
to cease and the slow erosion I felt,
being older than you, invades you too,
you'll come to see that an image of the desert
is the memory of water, like remembering

when we were walking in beautiful Barcelona
and you said you thought trees were gods
because they were rooted in earth
and flew in the air and magically made food
out of light and made the air we breathe.

I was stunned how you could open up a God-space
just like that. Like when my two-year-old dug holes
in the yard and fit his face into each of them to see,
as he explained, if he could find where the darkness
came from. Then you asked me why I never prayed.

I believe whatever disappears or survives
or comes into being is a prayer that's already
been answered, and that we feel alone
because we won't let go of what is gone
or changed or hasn't happened yet.

Waking this morning with my arms around you,
the dogs snoring, and a mourning dove cooing,
I felt I awoke in a peaceable kingdom
where the fear of death turned inside-out
into a love for life. If I prayed, I'd pray for that for you.

Road Work

> *Everything [important] is* kitsch.
> —Yehuda Amichai

After four days of ripping across the Bible Belt, boxed-in
at 70 mph between trailer trucks, just for the fun of it
I press my garage door opener and imagine pulling inside
and hearing Sam's soulful howling and little Sufi woofing
like a three-pack-a-day old lady coughing, and you laughing
as if someone were shaking out a bag of piccolo notes.

Today I miss you like a wild guess. Like the way we met.
No, more like me explaining to my two-year-old granddaughter
that those mounds of cotton rolling across heaven up there
are actually made of water. I wave as I pass beneath
a highway camera as if somebody might wave back.

Remember last week when I told you I could feel my mortality,
palpably; how that made things that were once important to me
like money and sex and the power of feeling and me
taking my whole life to learn how to tell about it all
seem like a fistful of lint and pennies
when the machine I'm kicking at says it wants quarters?

Well forget about that. Today I'm feeling like a small man
made larger by lip-syncing to Tammy Wynette who's whining
about how the only things she had left, a dish and a spoon, ran away
together. That's when I realized her purple-patched broken heart
is actually made up of millions of deeply felt lives
sleeping them off in a trashed-out trailer up on cinder blocks.

She made me feel that learning to line dance, doing the two-step,
and weeping along with what's being extruded from the radio
don't seem half as cheesy as the staticky nothingness that happens
when your number's up. That's when I thought of the colonoscopy
I had before I left you, how it was actually kind of sad
because being knocked out I couldn't feel a thing.

Now I know that's not a very romantic thing to say. But it's as close
as us men folk get to saying, Heck, I miss you, darling.
Hey, there goes a fat guy someone hired to wave an orange flag at me.
Heck, I miss everybody.

102

103

Acknowledgments

The American Poetry Review: "Beggar's Cup," "Shell Game," "Sleep Walking," "Nose Job," "Dark Matter," and "Catwalk, Flag Part, Tent Flap, and Shoe Tongue"

Café Review: "The Golden Years," "In," "Doggie's Day Out," "Art," "Desert is the Memory of Water," "Snapshots of Prague," "Paradise," "Life on Earth," and "Cloud, Backlit"

Callaloo: "Any Minute Now"

Charitan Review: "Really Fast Chicken," "Neighbors," "Treasure Hunt," "Intimacies of Cleaning," and "Black Loam"

Hunger Mountain: "Invisible Stones," "Same Sea," "American Bardo," "Human Flames," "There is Nothing in My Hands," and "Stone Koan"

The Langdon Review: "Someone Else's Shoes," "What the Old Master Said," "Fragments," "Nose Job," and "Dark Matter"

The New Ohio Review: "My Life," "Birth Day Party," and "Plans"

Oak Bend Review: "Necklace of Moss"

Platte Valley Review: "Intimacies of Cleaning," "Going Away Party," "*Mariscos*," and "Cholangiocarcinoma"

Poetry East: "The World's Highest Mountain"

SMU Magazine Online: "The Amnesiac's Memoir," "Art," "What It Takes," "Really Fast Chicken," "Cirrus," and "To-Do List"

The Texas Observer: "You are What You Don't Eat" and "Eating Grief"

Texas Review: "There is Nothing in My Hands," "Riding Shotgun in My Life," "Gold Watch," "Cirrus," and "This"

"Life on Earth" (as "Summers on Earth") also appeared in *Joyous Noise, An Anthology of American Poems and Prayers* (Autumn House, 2006), ed., Robert Strong.

"Desert is the Memory of Water": Thanks to the writer Jim Cornfield ("Living History," *Continental*, 8/08) for this poem's title.

Jack also wished to express sincere thanks to Southern Methodist University and The University of North Carolina at Wilmington's Creative Writing Department for their generosity in allowing him the time in which to complete this book.

photo by Thea Temple

The career of poet Jack Myers (b. 1941 - d. 2009) spanned five decades, during which time he authored/edited 19 books of and about poetry, established himself as an inspirational reader, and fathered four children. His many awards include two NEA Fellowships and the 1985 National Poetry Series selected by Seamus Heaney, who described Myers' work as "wise in the pretense of just fooling around." A much-loved teacher, Jack helped hundreds of poets find their voice through the creative writing programs at Vermont College and Southern Methodist University, as well as during residencies from Idaho to Prague. From 1993-95, he served as co-Vice-President for AWP and co-founded, with his wife, Thea Temple, The Writer's Garret literary center in Dallas; in 2003-04 he was selected to be the Poet Laureate of Texas.

New Issues Poetry

Seth Abramson, *Northerners*
Vito Aiuto, *Self-Portrait as Jerry Quarry*
James Armstrong, *Monument in a Summer Hat*
Claire Bateman, *Clumsy; Leap*
Sandra Beasley, *Theories of Falling*
Kevin Boyle, *A Home for Wayward Girls*
Jason Bredle, *Standing in Line for the Beast*
Jericho Brown, *Please*
Michael Burkard, *Pennsylvania Collection Agency*
Christopher Bursk, *Ovid at Fifteen*
Anthony Butts, *Fifth Season; Little Low Heaven*
Kevin Cantwell, *Something Black in the Green Part of Your Eye*
Gladys Cardiff, *A Bare Unpainted Table*
Stacie Cassarino, *Zero at the Bone*
Kevin Clark, *In the Evening of No Warning*
Cynie Cory, *American Girl*
Peter Covino, *Cut Off the Ears of Winter*
James D'Agostino, *Nude with Anything*
Jim Daniels, *Night with Drive-By Shooting Stars*
Keith Ekiss, *Pima Road Notebook*
Joseph Featherstone, *Brace's Cove*
Lisa Fishman, *The Deep Heart's Core Is a Suitcase*
Beckian Fritz Goldberg, *Reliquary Fever: New and Selected Poems*
Noah Eli Gordon, *A Fiddle Pulled from the Throat of a Sparrow*
Robert Grunst, *The Smallest Bird in North America*
Paul Guest, *The Resurrection of the Body and the Ruin of the World*
Robert Haight, *Emergences and Spinner Falls*
Judy Halebsky, *Sky=Empty*
Mark Halperin, *Time as Distance*
Myronn Hardy, *Approaching the Center; The Headless Saints*
Brian Henry, *Graft*
Edward Haworth Hoeppner, *Rain Through High Windows*
Cynthia Hogue, *Flux*
Jeff Hoffman, *Journal of American Foreign Policy*
Joan Houlihan, *The Mending Worm*
Christine Hume, *Alaskaphrenia*
Mark Irwin, *Tall If*
Josie Kearns, *New Numbers*
David Keplinger, *The Clearing; The Prayers of Others*

Maurice Kilwein Guevara, *Autobiography of So-and-So:
   Poems in Prose*
Ruth Ellen Kocher, *When the Moon Knows You're Wandering;
   One Girl Babylon*
Gerry LaFemina, *The Window Facing Winter*
Steve Langan, *Freezing*
Lance Larsen, *Erasable Walls*
David Dodd Lee, *Abrupt Rural; Downsides of Fish Culture*
Lisa Lewis, *Vivisect*
M.L. Liebler, *The Moon a Box*
Alexander Long, *Vigil*
Deanne Lundin, *The Ginseng Hunter's Notebook*
Barbara Maloutas, *In a Combination of Practices*
Joy Manesiotis, *They Sing to Her Bones*
Sarah Mangold, *Household Mechanics*
Gail Martin, *The Hourglass Heart*
Malinda Markham, *Having Cut the Sparrow's Heart*
Justin Marks, *A Million in Prizes*
David Marlatt, *A Hog Slaughtering Woman*
Louise Mathias, *Lark Apprentice*
Khaled Mattawa, *Tocqueville*
Gretchen Mattox, *Buddha Box; Goodnight Architecture*
Carrie McGath, *Small Murders*
Paula McLain, *Less of Her; Stumble, Gorgeous*
Lydia Melvin, *South of Here*
Sarah Messer, *Bandit Letters*
Wayne Miller, *Only the Senses Sleep*
Malena Mörling, *Ocean Avenue*
Julie Moulds, *The Woman with a Cubed Head*
Jack Myers, *The Memory of Water*
Carsten René Nielsen, *The World Cut Out with Crooked Scissors*
Marsha de la O, *Black Hope*
C. Mikal Oness, *Water Becomes Bone*
Bradley Paul, *The Obvious*
Jennifer Perrine, *The Body Is No Machine*
Katie Peterson, *This One Tree*
Jon Pineda, *The Translator's Diary*
Donald Platt, *Dirt Angels*
Elizabeth Powell, *The Republic of Self*
Margaret Rabb, *Granite Dives*
Rebecca Reynolds, *Daughter of the Hangnail; The Bovine Two-Step*
Martha Rhodes, *Perfect Disappearance*
Beth Roberts, *Brief Moral History in Blue*
John Rybicki, *Traveling at High Speeds* (expanded second edition

Mary Ann Samyn, *Inside the Yellow Dress; Purr; Beauty Breaks In*
Ever Saskya, *The Porch is a Journey Different from the House*
Maxine Scates, *Undone*
Mark Scott, *Tactile Values*
Hugh Seidman, *Somebody Stand Up and Sing*
Heather Sellers, *The Boys I Borrow*
Martha Serpas, *Côte Blanche*
Diane Seuss-Brakeman, *It Blows You Hollow*
Elaine Sexton, *Sleuth; Causeway*
Patty Seyburn, *Hilarity*
Marc Sheehan, *Greatest Hits*
Heidi Lynn Staples, *Guess Can Gallop*
Phillip Sterling, *Mutual Shores*
Angela Sorby, *Distance Learning*
Matthew Thorburn, *Subject to Change*
Russell Thorburn, *Approximate Desire*
Rodney Torreson, *A Breathable Light*
Lee Upton, *Undid in the Land of Undone*
Robert VanderMolen, *Breath*
Martin Walls, *Small Human Detail in Care of National Trust*
Patricia Jabbeh Wesley, *Before the Palm Could Bloom: Poems of Africa*